THE BIRTH OF JESUS

Illustrated by Tony Morris

Brimax · Newmarket · England

Long ago in a small town called Nazareth, there lived a young girl named Mary. At that time many people had forgotten about God, so He decided to send a little child to live and grow up among the people. This little child would teach them about God.

God knew that Mary loved him, so He chose her to be the mother of His child. He sent an angel called Gabriel to tell Mary about the baby. She was very frightened when she saw the angel standing near her.

The angel smiled and said, "Do not be afraid, Mary. God has sent me to tell you some good news. Soon you will have a baby. It will be a boy and his name will be Jesus. He will be a holy child, for he will be the Son of God."

A carpenter called Joseph also lived in Nazareth. He loved Mary and wanted to take care of her and the baby. So Joseph took Mary to be his wife.

King Herod decided that he wanted everyone to be counted, so Mary and Joseph had to return to the place where they were born. It was a very long way to go. Mary rode on a donkey and Joseph walked along beside her. At last they arrived and tried to find somewhere to stay.

They were very tired and they both needed to rest. Joseph knocked on the door of an inn. "Have you a bed for the night?" Joseph asked the inn-keeper. "My wife is very tired. We have come a long way."

"I am very sorry," said the inn-keeper, shaking his head. "There are no rooms left here. The only thing I can offer you is the stable, if you don't mind sharing with the animals. It is warm and dry."

"Thank you," said Joseph. "That will do very well."

They followed the inn-keeper, who led them out to the stable. Later that night, in the stable with the animals, the baby Jesus was born.

Mary had nothing for the baby to wear, so she wrapped him in strips of cloth. There was nowhere for the baby to sleep, so Joseph placed some soft straw in a manger and made a little bed for the baby Jesus. Mary gently laid the baby down in the manger to sleep.

Outside, on a nearby hillside, some shepherds were looking after their sheep. It was a cold, dark night, so they all sat close to the fire trying to keep warm. Suddenly, a great light shone in the sky and an angel stood before them.

They were all frightened, but the angel said, "Do not be afraid, for I have some good news to tell you. Tonight the Lord Jesus has been born. You must go to him. Follow the bright star and it will lead you to the stable where he lies. Then suddenly the sky was filled with angels singing.
  "Glory to God in heaven,
  Peace on earth
  And Joy to all men."

The shepherds left at once and followed the star which led them to the stable. They took their sheep with them. The shepherds knocked on the stable door and Joseph let them in. All the shepherds knelt beside the baby because they knew he was very special. Then the shepherds went to the town to tell everyone about the birth of the Lord Jesus.

Some wise men had been watching the stars. They knew a great king was to be born. At last they saw the bright star, which they followed across many lands. They thought they would find the new king in a palace, so they went to the palace of King Herod.

King Herod was angry to hear of this new king. He said to the wise men, "When you find this king, you must tell me where he is so I can worship him, too." In fact Herod wanted to kill Jesus.

The wise men finally found Jesus in a stable, asleep in the manger. They knew at once that he was the king they had been waiting for. Each wise man had a gift for Jesus which they laid down beside him — gold, frankincense and myrrh.

That night the wise men had a strange dream. In the dream, God told them not to return to King Herod as he meant to harm Jesus.
The next morning the wise men began their journey home. They did not return to the palace of King Herod.

When the wise men had gone, Mary thought again about what the angel had said to her. She picked Jesus up and held him close. She knew that Jesus was very special, and that his birth would always be remembered as a time of great joy and happiness.

All these appear in the pages of the story.
Can you find them?

angel

inn-keeper

manger

Joseph